GUIDE TO IMMIGRATING

AND

SETTLING IN CANADA

By

Guggu V

Immigrating to Canada

Introduction

This is a comprehensive guide which will help every aspirant who wishes to Immigrate to Canada to be a successful Canadian. Every aspect from obtaining the Canadian 'Green Card' to preparation and arrival in Canada has been researched from various sources and forums and is presented in an easy to read format. This guide will help you to avoid any setbacks and prepare you leading towards a smooth landing in Canada.

The Application

Every individual who wishes to immigration to Canada always asks the same query being time and again. [1] How to Apply? [2] Where to apply? [3] Do we get a Consultant or Immigration Attorney or go DIY route?

Under the present 'fast track' system, the PR processing of FSW is quite 'simple & straight'. We actually don't need an 'agent', unless something is bothering us, viz. problem cases, previous rejections, lack of time, some complexities etc. Even under that duress, we can still do it ourselves. Today, for processing our FSW cases all we need is the awesome CIC website www.cic.gc.ca which has a detailed Guide.

Note that most consultants would just be rendering 'courier & typing' services. And when we need real 'consultancy' we'll find them lacking & inaccessible. Secondly, they are prone to delaying our cases. Thirdly, we'll yet be running into these Forums for getting your queries answered. It doesn't mean all are bad, but most are. And for just that is spending our hard-earned greenbacks on them justified? I feel "No".

Here's how we can go about it...

How do we send the Application?
Initially we send the Apps (+Processing Fees + some Docs [only]) to the CIO-NS, wherever we are, whatever our CHC may be. Thereafter, once we get the AOR+120 days letter, we send the complete docs (+Copies of One Set of the 'original' apps +the RPRF) to the local Visa Office (CHC). And wait for further instructions. For more information, see below information.

Instruction Guide [IMM EG7000]

For details & complete procedure on the above please refer to the CIC Instruction Guide here:
http://www.cic.gc.ca/english/information/applications/guides/EG7TOC.asp

Application Forms
The full set of application forms are given here:
http://www.cic.gc.ca/english/pdf/kits/forms/IMM5612E.PDF

The Process in a Nutshell
Stage-1: [CIO stage] Send Initial Apps + Processing Fees to CIO-NS > Eligibility Check > Issue of AOR+120 days Letter >

Stage-2: [CHC stage onwards] Send Full Docs + RPRF to the Local Visa Office > File on Queue > e-Cas: "Received by Visa Office" > Qualitative Check + PSDEC > Issue of 2nd AOR > Background Check > Issue of Additional docs Request [if any] > 1st BF'D > e-Cas: "In Process" > Send Addnl. Docs > Issue of Med Request > 2nd BF'D >

Stage-3: Meds Sent > e-Cas: "Medical Results Recd." > Issue of PPR** > Send Passport/s > Security Check > Visa/s Stamped > e-Cas: "Decision Made" >

Stage-4: Return of 'Stamped' Passport/s+ COPR > landing at the POE > e-Cas: "Completed".

Timeframe for the 'entire' Process:
Let whatever the Consultants or their Adverts say. The total timeframe [from 1st application to case completion'] is 6-18 months. Average is 12 months. Many get it within 8-10 months. This timeframe is not one CHC specific as it's for all CHCs., Most of us will 'compete' the process in 1 year unless there are any 'red flags' in our case that delays the Background or Security Checks.

Note:
RPRF can be sent anytime during the process. However, it is good to send it early. Meds & PPR are sometimes clubbed together.

There would be people who would find a Consultant quite handy, but overall, are we so naive today? Are we not 'internet-savvy? Can't we devote few days [taken off from work] to read the guide & fill-out the forms? Then, where's the problem in avoiding a Consultant unless we are okay with spending our $$$.

However, whether to go with a Consultant or DIY is surely a personal choice & that is debatable.

Background & Security Checks

Note: Our Background Check comprises of 2 parts:
1. The Standard Documentation Checks,
2. The Security & Criminality Checks.

Standard Documentation Checks:

Our background check is done at the CHC stage. It commences the moment our file gets the 1st BFD by the VO. An indicator of which is the e-CAS that shows "In Progress". All docs been checked & our NOC being tallied against the MI, if the VO finds our case 'eligible' for Canadian PR, the file becomes 'Accepted'; and then it goes for standard background checks, viz. experience, qualifications, adaptability, qualitative considerations etc.

The process involves many things. If our case file is well presented and the enclosures vouch the quality-quantity, adequate POF docs etc., there might not be a requirement of 'actually' calling the employers, references etc. The VOs have a way with that, they are experienced enough to ascertain the logical disposition of our case. But, if there are any concerns of his/her, s/he is likely to ask for additional docs, do further scrutiny vide any means [calling, visiting etc.] & might ask for an Interview.

Culmination: When 'fully' satisfied, we get the 'Medical Request'.
Timeframe: Can be anything around 3-8* months, for the 'fast track' system (Avg. 4-5 months).
eCAS: Continues to Show 'In Process'.
 *The older system has a queue, thus can be longer.

Security & Criminality Checks:

A part of the background checks is the 'Security Check'. It commences after our med results are submitted to the CHC. This is a major activity -mainly concerning our 'safe inclusion' into the Canadian Soil; i.e. Political, Socio-Economical, Anti-Social disposition, perceived threat to Canada's integrity etc. This gets us the SDEC, CDEC & SECCRIM.

This is a serious & time-consuming stage, involving many agencies, including CSIS, Interpol, NASC, Database Checking & touch-base with Local Police. Many things are considered here. The number of countries visited, Applicant coming from 'certain' countries, ex-Servicemen [including Law Enforcement services], Prolonged stay in a country without sufficient docs to prove cause, frequent traveling to certain nations, your Name, Inter-Religion/Nationality Marriages etc.

If everything is simple & straight, the file soon gets into the 'final review' stage. If there are any 'red flags', our case goes into a 'spin'. Then our file might go to the local Police/CID agencies; the outcome/timeframe of which is beyond the control of CIC. And thereby the timeframe can be anything [sometimes beyond 1year]. But, usually this stage should be over by 5 months max. However, a point to be noted is that we can also be called for an Interview [at this stage], due to this reason.

Culmination: Only upon security clearance we receive the PPR.
Timeframe: Around 2-6 months. Average 3 months. [With new system, sometimes PPR is clubbed with Meds]
eCAS: Still 'In Process', but 'Med Results Recd.' inside.

Lots of us have got the visas lately and we are now having some doubt about our 'choice of landing', after being on this great forum & having surfed enough regarding various Canadian cities. Thus, the question, "Should I land in the city mentioned in my Application/COPR, or can I go to another Canadian city"?

As a federal skilled worker, we can chose any POE in Canada & complete our landing formalities, regardless of the destination mentioned in our Apps or the COPR, except Quebec.

Canada's Immigration Laws provide for a 2 step process for our visa applications:
>Step-1. The CIC/CHCs carry out stage One (read our apps processing system).
>Step-2. This is carried out by an Immigration Officer at the POE.

Regarding Step-1, we are already familiar. This is how we get our PR Visas. For the Step-2 (at POE) however, landing is our "Right". Though not an 'automatic right', we must still satisfy the officer at the POE that our entry is permissible: A12 (1), called the 'Verification of PR', outlined in Sections 19(1) & (2) of the Act. But, another thing is also involved in this Step-2, called 'Completion of the Record of Landing' for admission into Canada, which is obligatory.

For this "Record of Landing", 'admissibility' is not affected by our choice of POE. All it's needed is to fill up certain forms, specifically the PR Card form (IMM 5444E), wherein we have to provide an address for card delivery. This can be anywhere, beyond the POE. This is how newcomers with COPR destination as Montreal-Quebec drive through the POE of Sarnia, Bluewater Bridge. There are many other examples, but for brevity I just chose one.

There is only 'one' catch though. For Quebec, although any FSW would be allowed to enter thru a Quebec POE, they cannot complete the 'Record of Landing' here. And would have to further drive/fly to another province (any) to report to its Immigration Officer for the 'completion' of record of landing. This is because Quebec needs the CSQ certificate to complete this procedure which is only for a Quebec PR applicant; however, it is not vice-versa i.e. a Quebec PR applicant can do all the formalities in any other Canadian POE.

Finally anyone of us FSWs can land in any Canadian POE, irrespective of what's written in our apps or the COPR.

Which City to Land?

For FSW without AEO & friends/relatives my opinion is <u>TORONTO</u>.
-It has a bigger job basket, for any occupation. Thus, the share is bigger, so the opportunities are larger.
-Weather wise, it is not that bad. It is perfectly manageable even in winters or summers.
-Cost of living wise, quite ok too -quite competitive v/s the other deciding factors.
-The highest minority populace. People are extremely tolerant to race, color, creed, faith, etc.
-Land there first, take a 'survival job', which will be easier here & move to any city after getting the choice job.
-Important: It's not the profession of a newcomer, but the initial survival that would be the decider for a city.

<u>VANCOUVER</u>:
Very aptly said by that it's the best city weather wise & has a charmed beauty. Quite nice minority populace, and yes Indians rock here. But, it's better <u>avoided</u>.
-No or minimal jobs today for any field. *(Note: the winter Olympics thing is temporary)*
-The costliest city to settle down.
-Housing cost is sky rocketing.
-Not at all a good choice for a newcomer, without AOE or friends/relatives support.
-What's the point of all that beauty, if you do not have <u>money</u> in your pocket?

<u>CALGARY-EDMONTON CORRIDOR</u>:
Very nicely coming-up. Weather is cold, but adjustable *[Edmonton needs adaptation though]*.

Has the 'Rockies' to enhance its beauty. It is a perfect <u>alternative</u> to Vancouver. But:
-Newcomers should take it as a 2nd choice to Toronto. Due to the factors I said under Toronto.
-Damn good for establishing a business. *(No provincial tax)*
-Essentially a befitting place for Oil & Gas sector, which also makes other jobs <u>available</u> in their HOs.
-But <u>remember</u> again: For newcomer jobs, take **Toronto** as POE.

There is nothing wrong in other Canadian cities. But this advice is meant for newcomers, looking for <u>instant jobs</u>, not for business; and for those who <u>do not</u> have an AOE or friends/relatives to initially assist. Else, any other city has its own merits/demerits.

When should we Land?

After getting the PR visa, we are supposed to complete our 'record of landing', on or before the Visa Expiry Date [mentioned on the visa]. The visa Expiry Date is related to EITHER*:
a) 1yr. from the meds, or
b) Passport expiry date of the PA or anyone of his/her accompanying Dependents
*Whichever of the above 2 is earlier.

WHO SHOULD LAND FIRST:

It is the obligation of the PA to 'land' first and can be 'along with' one or more or all the accompanying family members. Let it be clear that the PA's dependents CANNOT land first.

PROCEDURE AT THE POE:

Irrespective of which city we chose to land, the 'landing' per se, is a simple process. Before disembarking the aircraft we'll be provided with a 'Disembarkation Card/Form'. We take that form & first go to the 'Passport Control'.

At the Passport Control:

Here we need to inform the IO that we have come to do our 'landing'. The IO will check our Disembarkation Card and our passport/s & visa. They will then direct us to "Newly Landed Immigrants' Counter".

At the Immigration Counter:

The IO here will scrutinize our Passport/s & COPRs. He would [sometimes may not] ask to see our POF. Most of the times, the officer will not count the 'actual' money & will accept what we say. No false pretensions there. They will then fill some portions of the COPR & ask us to sign it, wherein it'll be attached on our passport. We'll be asked to fill-in the 'PR Card Application Form' & give an address where our PR cards will be forwarded within 3-6 weeks. Thereby, they would 'Welcome us to Canada' and direct us to another office.

At the Services Canada Office:

The Services Canada section is for assisting the Newcomers' settlement moves. Here we'll get lots of books/pamphlets, that'll provide all the crucial info on Canada and our Settlement plan here. From here will be directed to the CBSA counter.

At the CBSA [Customs] Office:

This is an important location. We are required to present (1) List of Items Accompanying; (2) List of Goods to follow; (3) Currency Declaration [We'd have to 'declare' any amount of $10K or more]. Lists-1 & 2 must be brought in 2 copies, one would be retained by CBSA and the 2nd copy will be returned back to us. We'll need the 2nd copy when our shipments come-in.

Note: [1] If we are not bringing-in any goods later, we don't need the 'goods to follow list'. [2] At a random the CBSA might 'actually' check the POF here. Thus, no complacency is acceptable. [3] If there is 'jewelry' involved, do not forget to bring 'Printed Photographs' of the same (details later).

All the officers are extremely friendly, very understanding, cheerful and helpful. We'll encounter 'Welcome to Canada' many a times. If all the docs are pre-printed & available with us; and there is not much of a queue, we will be out of the airport in 40 mins-1hr. flat which includes the walk-distance, baggage collection etc.

FORMS REQUIRED FOR THE 'LANDING':
Even if you stay ONLY for a day at Canada, you will need the following:

1. Passport with stamped Visa.
2. COPR (IMM 5292B)
3. POF. [For cases "without" AEO & family class] (Details below)
4. Passport size photos. -2 or 3 for PRC (may not be needed, but good to have)
5. PR Card Application (IMM 5444E). -carry it filled pre-printed, for ease
6. Goods to Follow List (Form B4 / B4A). -carry it filled pre-printed, for ease
7. Goods Accompanying List. -as above, a table of things you are carrying on person (value & totaled)
Forms required later
8. SIN Card Apps Form (NAS 2120). -Not needed at the A/port [later at Services Canada]
9. Kids Immunization Record - Not needed at the Airport [later for School Admission]
10. If you are driving your car -read below

NOTE: The more you are organized beforehand, the better 1st impression you deliver and the IO/CBSA officer shall be happier. (BTW: smooth & fast processing). You'll be out faster. Go to your accommodation & relax for the day, you had a long journey, haven't you?

SHORT STAY ACCOMMODATION:
For sure you must arrange a 'short-stay' accommodation prior to your landing. The necessity of which cannot be overemphasized more. If you have friends/relatives, they can be approached for the same, if you do not have anyone, the following is recommended:

Toronto:
1) http://www.staystudio6.com/
*Provides airport pick-up services and used by many satisfactorily.

Calgary:
Not many such places are available. Look for local listings.

Vancouver:
a) http://www.budgetpathotel.bc.ca/
b) http://www.ywcahotel.com/

Some other important sites on Vancouver are:
1) http://www.welcomebc.ca
2) http://www.rentbc.com

NOTE: Except for people with enough $$$ to spend, avoid Hotels & Motels. They are far costlier. Also, if you must take a hotel, avoid the ones close to the Airport -for obvious reasons.

HOUSE RENTAL:
The best way to do house hunting [long-term accommodation.] is to land at Canada & then start searching. Word of mouth & Bulletin Boards are a great 'real-time' source. However, we cannot condone the importance of the web. Some of the good sites [there are many] could be:
a) http://www.hometrader.ca (Good site)
b) http://www.capreit.com (Property Management Services)
c) http://www.kjiji.ca/ (Good Classifieds site)
d) http://www.mls.ca (Mother of all)

Money: Proof of Landing Funds

What Proofs Are Acceptable?
If you are carrying more than C$10,000, tell a Canadian official when you arrive in Canada. If you do not tell an official, you may be fined or put in prison. These funds could be in the form of:

• Cash

• Securities in bearer form (for e.g., stocks, bonds, debentures, treasury bills) or

• Negotiable instruments in bearer form (for e.g., B/drafts, Cheques, TCs or MOs).

Source: http://www.cic.gc.ca/english/immigrate/skilled/funds.asp

How Much Funds Can I Carry?
There is no Max limit. We can take Millions, if we can prove its legitimate source & declare anything at/or more than $10,000 [that's the CBSA regulation]. There is a Minimum limit though. We must carry at least or more than what CIC requirement states, for the no. of persons in the family [accompanying].

Tax & Duties Component:
The funds we bring inside Canada are Non-Taxable. It is only the 'interest' earned on that which is taxed. The moment our funds start accruing interest [while lying in a Canadian Bank a/c] the bank will start deducting tax 'on source'. The same applies for any 'investment' in Canada that we make with these funds.

How much needed to Show at the Airport/POE:
No. of persons........... Funds Required-CAD

1 .... $11,086

2 .... $13,801

3 .... $16,967

4 .... $20,599

5 .... $23,364

6....................... $26,350

7 or more............. $29,337

Is it necessary to carry the P.O.F. while 'Landing'?
100%. A part of the 'Record of Landing' "Interview" is to ensure 'sustainability' in Canada by the applicant. The IO must ensure that you carry enough funds [based on LICO] which will help you settle easily, w/out any burden on Canadian Social Services. Remember, except for 'refugees' under the Refugees Protection Act, Canada doesn't offer financial assistance for any other categories of applicants.

Irrespective of the no. of family members performing the 1st landing, the entire

POF [as per the chart above] must be shown to the IO at the POE. Subsequent 'landings' by the 'accompanying dependents' do not need to show the POF.

That means, whether the PA alone or one or more of his family members are 'landing' for the 1st time, the above funds are required. It's another matter whether the IO at the POE doesn't ask for it. But, without the POF our entry can be **'Denied'**.

Bank Statement/s as POF:
The fact remains that we will actually need those monies once we land. Under average, & usual circumstances -the POF described by the CIC is a necessity to survive in Canada, without a job, for approx. 6 months. Thus, in all earnestness we 'must' carry the 'landing funds' in a 'liquid' format* -easily accessible anytime upon landing.

Now, not all Bank Statements would be acceptable for 'landing'. There are instances when a Bank Statement was negated and the applicant was denied entry. Most 3rd World Bank's statements will not be acceptable.

However, the statements of banks from UK, US, Norway, ANZ, etc., were accepted in quite a few cases. Also, statements of International Banks [having a presence in Canada] were acceptable, viz. HSBC, Stanchart, RBC etc. But again, one case stated that their Citibank Statement was not accepted.

Now, here's a dichotomy. Our landing is supposed to be one of the most beautiful experiences of our lifetime. We have given our entirety to this process, didn't we? Something we had been looking forward to -for quite some time now. What if a particular IO refuses to accept our bank statement?

Well, we have learnt that many of the bank's statement they do accept, but what if? And then, would we be running around towards all the possible hierarchy in the CBSA at the POE for a solution -which might come by, for sure? But won't that mar the thrills of our 'long-awaited-anticipated' first-foot into the Canadian soil? Do we take that chance? Is it that important to carry the bank statement than expect to come-out of the airport, with the family & kids, in 30-45 minutes, smoothly?

*I recommend carrying them in 1) Some Cash, 2) TCs & 3)a Bank Draft [it takes about 30+ days to cash that]. -all the 3 formats [only], No Bank Statements.

Note: Also to reiterate that all Immigration Consultants will tell you to carry 'only' one or more of the 3 above. They wouldn't advise you to take a bank statement, why? -Check-it out with some of them.

Banking

Though most international banks operate in Canada, the 5 Canadian Banks are presumably the best, in terms of their presence, availability & location of ATM machines, branches etc.:

1) CIBC
2) BMO
3) Scotiabank
4) TD Bank
5) RBC

Besides, you can also pre-open a Canadian Bank account from your home country through Scotiabank, SBI & *ICICI Bank.

*ICICI Bank offers one of the cheapest a/c charges. But unfortunately, both ICICI & SBI have very limited presence in Canada.

Most of the 5 Canadian Banks have a Newcomers Program to Canada where you get free banking services for up to a year. Under this program, the bank waives your monthly service fees and also gives you a secured credit card which you can use to build your credit history in Canada. Check with your bank on the Newcomers Program and get started with building your credit history.

Airline Recommendations

Usually BA & KLM change places frequently for their "lowest fares" to Canada. More often it'd be BA [especially from the UK, Dubai, Europe & the Gulf sector]. You can also ask your travel agent to select between multiple carriers to provide multiple-halt choices. But, from the UK actually that might not be required.

However, personal choice prevails. Sometimes other carriers place envious promotions too. Emirates has recently commenced the A380 [Dreamliner] service. And all their flights are 'long-haul' -Non Stop.

NOTE: If our $$$ are a consideration, avoid 'non-stop' flights. They obviously are costlier. A single-stop flight is highly recommended. Also, we might avoid travel agents as well, the 'online' reservation of all the prominent carriers are absolutely good. I did mine through BA & it was fantastic. Paid, printed and became an 'Executive Club' member -all thru the net. The e-ticket shall be delivered, on-the-spot, in your email in-box.

PR Cards (PRC)

Your PR Card application (IMM 5444E) shall be done at the POE itself. It is part of the PR package [free] and the photos & details will be the same as you supplied for the PPR. Our PR Cards come back to us via regular post mail, in 3-6 weeks, avg. 4 weeks. It is 'advisable' for one to stay in Canada for at least 45 days, collect our PRC and then return back [if you must].

If you leave the country before it arrives, you'll have to make arrangements for its collection & forward delivery to you, overseas, thru a friend/relative [Not a Recommended Action], however, done all the time by people. But there is a danger of losing it in transit. And if that happens, we'll have a tedious process to get new ones made.

How to Enter Canada without a PR Card:

As per IATA & CBSA regulations, we cannot enter Canada without a PRC. However, if we are entering thru a Border Post by road, it doesn't matter -our COPR is enough for entry/exit. But, if we are travelling by an airline & boarding/entering through an airport we will not be permitted. At the embarkation port itself we will be stopped by the airline staff.

The process in such cases is to apply for a 'PRTD-A31 (3)' [Temporary 'PR Travel Document'] at the local CHC [abroad]. It costs Ca$50. Details of it are provided at the 'Manual for Permanent Resident Card' (ENF 27).

Procedure Of PR Card Application:

http://www.cic.gc.ca/english/pdf/kits/guides/5445E.PDF

NOTE: The PRC is probably the 'most important' document after we are thru with our PR application process. This is valid for 5 yrs. First time: Free; Renewals cost $50/card and can be renewed every 5 yrs. (if you don't apply for Citizenship of Canada)

SIN Cards

After 'landing' we'll have to visit the nearest Services Canada Office for the SIN Card. We get the SIN No. immediately as a 'print-out' -signed & stamped upon applying, the same day, the same time. That'd suffice for all our further actions in Canada, via Job Search, Bank a/c, House Hunting etc. The card shall come to us in approx. 3 weeks. For its collection -ditto applies as above, for the PR Cards.

NOTE: Remember, we don't need the SIN Card for anything. We need only the SIN No. which we'll get the same time as we apply for it. It'd be wise to visit Services Canada Office the very next day upon arrival.

IMPORTANT NOTE:
Both PR Card & SIN Cards are Federal documents. Meaning, there is one card for the entire nation -Canada.

Health Cards & Canadian Health Care System

Health is a provincial matter. It is NOT FEDERAL. Thus, if you change provinces, you'll have to AGAIN get that province's Health Card. And again the waiting period*shall apply. Off course, a previous province's health card remains valid for few days/months in another province, but not all benefits could be availed.

Is our Health Care Free in Canada?

In a non-technical sense [generally speaking], **yes** -it is **"Free"**. However, technically it is indirectly charged to us vide the various forms of taxes that we pay against almost everything in Canada. But, overall it is fairly a good system, well managed and an envious one to many nations.

How the Health Care is delivered?

Though governed under the 'Canada Health Act' & Publicly Funded, the healthcare is not Federal but a provincial matter. Canada's health care system is actually an interlocking set of 10 provincial and 3 territorial health insurance plans. Known to Canadians as "Medicare," the system provides access to universal, comprehensive coverage for medically necessary hospital and physician services. These services are administered and delivered by the provincial & territorial governments, and are provided free of charge. The provincial and territorial governments fund health care services with assistance from the federal government.

What Medical Benefits we get for Free?

The medical benefits, called by any name [e.g. the *Medical Services Plan* (MSP)-in BC] provides the following benefits:

- Medically required services provided by a physician;
- Maternity care provided by a physician or a midwife;
- Medically required eye examinations provided by an ophthalmologist or optometrist;
- Diagnostic services, including x-rays and laboratory services, when ordered by a registered physician or surgeon;
- Dental and oral surgery, when medically required to be performed in hospital;
- Orthodontic services related to severe congenital facial abnormalities;
- **Complete Emergency Treatment.**

Which Services are not covered?

The Medicare does not cover for the following:

- Over-the-Counter Drugs/Medicines;
- Prescription drugs (e.g. PharmaCare
  http://www.health.gov.bc.ca/pharmacare/index.html);
- Services that are deemed not medically required, such as Cosmetic Surgery;

- Dental services, except as outlined under benefits;
- Routine eye examinations for persons 19 to 64 years of age;
- Eyeglasses, hearing aids, and other equipment or appliances;
- Massage therapy, naturopathy, physical therapy etc.;
- Preventive services and screening tests (e.g. routine annual physical exams);
- Services of counselors or psychologists;
- Medical examinations, certificates or tests required for:
  - Driving a motor vehicle
  - Employment
  - Life Insurance
  - School or University
  - Recreational and Sporting activities
  - Immigration purposes

How to Access the Medicare?
The health care is provided in 2 stages [generally speaking -though other complex issues are involved]. First, we head to the Family Physician, and then we may be referred for a Hospital care.

What Happens First (Primary Health Care Services)?
When Canadians need health care, they generally contact a primary health care professional, who could be a family doctor, nurse, nurse practitioner, physiotherapist, pharmacist, etc. Services provided at the first point of contact form the foundation of the health care system.

Primary health care services often include prevention and treatment of common diseases and injuries; basic emergency services; referrals to and coordination with other levels of care, such as hospital and specialist care; health promotion; primary maternity care etc.

What Happens Next (Secondary Services)?
A patient may be referred for specialized care at a hospital or at a long-term care facility. The majority of Canadian hospitals are operated by community boards of trustees, voluntary organizations or municipalities. Hospitals are paid through annual budgets negotiated with the provincial and territorial ministries of health.

How do you get a health card?
You can apply for a health card at the provincial ministry of health office in your city. You will find the address in the provincial government listings in your telephone book. Take with you your birth certificate, Canada Immigration visa (Record of Landing) and passport. Some provinces also request further documentation showing your name and address and your signature.

All members of your family must have their own coverage. Take their documents with you, and ask the government officer for information about registering them.

Who is eligible to receive a health card?

Canadian citizens and permanent residents are eligible in all provinces. Certain persons in Canada for a temporary period of time (e.g., temporary workers, holders of a Minister's permit, foreign students, and refugees whose status has been confirmed by the Immigration Refugee Board) are also eligible in some provinces. Essential health care services are available to refugee claimants through the Interim Federal Health Program at Citizenship and Immigration Canada.

How soon are you eligible?

Permanent residents are eligible immediately, except in British Columbia, Ontario and New Brunswick where there is a three-month waiting period. Persons in Canada temporarily and holding Immigration Canada documentation (e.g., temporary workers, holders of a Minister's permit and foreign students) have different waiting periods, depending on the province. For more information, contact the provincial ministry of health.

E.g.: If Calgary Is My Destination Should I Get The Health Card In Toronto?
If Calgary is your final destination, but you are 'initially' landing in Toronto for a few days stay [Permitted action] I suggest you should first land in Calgary [get the health card] and then visit Toronto. Why? Mainly because, you can get the Calgary health card immediately, but in Toronto you'll not. That Calgary health card will be valid in Toronto for a few days. Not the vice-versa. Secondly, if you land first in Toronto, you'll be staying w/out any health coverage.

Is your health card accepted throughout Canada?

For permanent residents, your health card is primarily for use in the province you live in. if you move to another province, reapply as soon as possible. There are waiting periods before you can be covered, although you are covered by the health plan of the province you left for a certain amount of time. If you are visiting another province, your card can be used in an emergency. Residents residing in a province for a temporary period should contact the provincial health insurance plan office in the province, of permanent residence for further clarification concerning their coverage throughout Canada.

*FUNDING FOR THE MEDICARE:
Each province administers a health care insurance plan for residents. These plans provide coverage from Primary medical care to Hospitalization to Emergency Response; and are available to all Canadian residents (including Permanent Residents).
· The method of paying for health care costs varies by province. In some areas, you are required to pay a monthly premium for coverage (i.e. Alberta). In other provinces, the cost is incorporated into the provincial tax system.
· Additional medical insurance for services not covered by provincial health care is also available through programs such as Blue Cross. These supplemental extended plans only cover over and above the basic coverage the provincial plans provide. (See http://www.bluecross.ca)

SOURCE & FURTHER READING:
1) http://en.wikipedia.org/wiki/Health_care_in_Canada
2) http://www.hc-sc.gc.ca/index-eng.php
3) http://users.eastlink.ca/~dhh/index_files/page0004.html
4) http://www.health.gov.bc.ca/msp/infoben/benefits.html

Do you need 'Temporary Health Insurance' while arriving in Canada?
Yes, you better!
I'm sure most would be aware by now that upon 'landing'...
1. We are not immediately covered under the Canadian Healthcare.
2. Most provinces (Except Alberta & Manitoba, as per my knowledge.) have a waiting period -of 3 months, before we are 'eligible' for the Medicare.
3. During this 3 months if we have a medical emergency -God save us!
It'll be a good idea to obtain the Travel Insurance from home country. For 2 reasons: [1] You are covered from day-1 even before landing. [2] In Canada it will be costlier & you'll be covered only from the day you apply. What if you get to do it later, as you'll be busy in the initial days? What if something goes wrong in between?

Why do we require one?
The Canadian health system is one of the best in the world, No doubts on that. But it is very expensive too*, if you are not covered under the Provincial Health Plan! Doctors in Canada charge hefty visitation fees; and if it's an emergency medical treatment, the costs simply shoot through the ceiling. Hospital care in Canada can cost your thousands of dollars on a daily basis and if you are unfortunate enough to meet with an accident or have other health issues -your Canadian dream could be a nightmare, before it dawns.

*Canada's health expenses rival the United States -as the most expensive in the world.
- Simple doctor visits cost .... approximately $150
- Ambulance .... approximately $250
- Critical hospital stay cost......... Around .... $3,500 per night
- Air ambulance....................... Around $20,000
- etc...

Sure, we might argue that we are perfectly fine -health wise, have been medically found fit for the immigrations process, haven't we? But what if we fall sick, or have an unexpected medical ailment, or need surgery, or meet with an accident... can we take that risk? 'Coz, if that happens -our 'landing funds' might just last a week to the max, sometimes might not either. And then, if not due to the sickness, the medical expenses itself could make us [financially] crippling.

So, where the answer lies?
To ensure personal safety, the answer lies is obtaining a "Temporary Health Insurance" which could be taken in either of the ways:
A. Pre-landing, from our homeland,
B. Post-landing, a.s.a.p. upon arrival in Canada.

A. Pre-Landing insurance: "Travel Insurance"
A Travel Health Insurance will provide an excellent safeguard against the extremely prohibitively costs of medical treatment in Canada which usually is very affordable and costs as little as $2 a day. There are many variants of the same in the market, while it'd be wise to obtain it from a reputed 'international agency', rather taking it from the cheapest 'fly-by night' insurance provider. The criteria being -it should have a presence 'in Canada', a No. to call in emergency & be able to get immediate advise/s. Some of such Travel Insurance Providers are:
1. AXA:
http://www.axa-gulf.com
2. IMG:
http://www.imglobal.com/insurance_plans.cfm?imgac=21263&frames=0&app_met hod=1&CFID=324496&CFTOKEN=4049b2fee42bf8df-A3F1550C-1F29-DFD5-1244E7E6281C111E
3. ICICI Lombard:
http://www.icicilombard.com/app/ilom-en/PersonalProducts/Travel/Individual_Overseas/Gold_Plan.aspx
4. Travel Guard Chartis:
http://www.travelguard.com/travelinsurance/travelmedical.asp

5. Allianz-Mondial:
http://www.mondial-assistance.ca/

CONDITIONS:
1. As this type of insurance is basically for holiday/business travel, thus we need to have a valid 'return air ticket' to obtain these. One way ticket would not qualify.
2. They cover everything -medicines to hospitalization, consultancy fees, Lab tests etc. you name it.
3. The hospitalization costs [including OPD later] would be paid directly by the insurer. But non-hospitalization ones need to claimed at the home country [not in Canada]*.
4. They are available [usually] for a maximum of 3 months. We should also take it for not less than 3 months [later the OHIP kicks-in].

*We can fill-up the Claim Form/s, attach the bills & send it back to a relative or friend to submit it to the Insurer. The claims are usually processed in 3-7 days max. S/he can collect it as well. If you obtain it through an Insurance Broker, [ideal choice] they'll do all the needful.

MY ADVICE:
This type of insurance is actually better. Also cheaper than the post-landing option. And we stand 'covered' from the port of embarkation itself. Besides, this insurance incorporates many other things like lost/delayed baggage, loss of passport, loss of monies, return of mortal remains etc. [details in the e.g., below]. Secondly, it might do us good to obtain the highest cover -the top most plan of any insurer... usually the one with $1Million.

B. Post-Landing Insurance: The "Visitor's to Canada" Plan
Generally, the coverage you need [post-landing] is the "visitors to Canada" Insurance Plans. Good news again is that this type of medical insurance is quite affordable as well. For example, a good individual coverage can be purchased for a 40 year old for $3-$5 per day, and an entire family can be covered for under$15 per day.

Medical Insurance is highly recommended for all foreign visitors to Canada, including new immigrants, says **CLHIA** (Canadian Life and Health Insurance Association). They recommend the following insurance companies:
1. Blue Cross - Tele: 1-800-873-2583
https://www.useblue.com/assurance-voyage/trouver-produit/liste-protections/visiteurs-canada1/visiteurs-canada-immigrants.en.html
2. ETFS - Tele: 1- 800-267-8834

http://www.etfsinc.com/product/individual/visitors.html
3. TIC - Tele: 1-800-387-4770
http://www.travelinsurance.ca/plans/visitorsGeneral.php
4. Canadian Banks*

*Many Canadian Banks also provide the said services to newcomers. For example, RBC.
http://www.rbcinsurance.com/travel/visitors-canada-plans.html

CONDITIONS:
1. Some insurance companies have rules and deadlines for buying these post-landing insurances.
2. For example, with some companies you will have to buy insurance within 7 days of arriving in Canada. While some allow you till 30 days.
3. Beyond 30 days there is hardly any Canadian insurance company which would sell this product.

MY ADVICE:
As a thumb rule, we 'must' obtain this type of insurance immediately upon arrival in Canada. Maybe get it the very next day itself. One never knows when fate or destiny may hit us hard, do we?

What Coverage do we expect from Temp Health Insurance?
-Complete medical treatment*
-Family Physician's Fees,
-Drugs or Medicines while hospitalized and a 'set limit' -if not hospitalized,
-Hospital Confinement -for Standard and sometimes semi-private rooms,
-Medical Services: Services of a legally licensed MD or Surgeon, Anesthetist, Registered Nurse,
-Lab tests, x-ray exams, other diagnostic tests,
-Licensed local air, land or sea ambulance
-Rental of hospital type bed, crutches, trusses, braces, splints or other approved prosthetic appliances,
-Emergency OPD (Out Patient) services
-Return of Deceased Body to Insured's' residence, or cost of cremation or burial at place of death
-Accidental Dental -set limits on costs of damage from accidental blow to the face
-Air Flight Accident (usually an option)
-24 hour Accidental Death or Dismemberment (usually an option)

*Some plans will though render Emergency basis only to cover sudden, unexpected, and unforeseeable circumstances [usually the lower premium ones].

A recommended Plan from the Gulf

From the Gulf, AXA offers a well-rounded plan, which has a better value for money, Premium vis-a-vis Coverage. It offers 2 plans for Worldwide coverage:

1. Travel Smart: Highest coverage -higher premium.

The best travel insurance product in the market to cover you with any medical and travel inconvenience for the complete peace of mind.

2. Travel Family: Good coverage -lower premium.

Comprehensive worldwide Family Cover under one single premium for insured person, spouse and unlimited number of children.

The Cover at a glance:	Travel Smart (USD)	Travel Family (USD)
-Emergency Medical	1,000,000	60,000
-Emergency Dental	400	1,000
-Emergency Transportation	Unlimited	60,000
-Repatriation of other insured person	Unlimited	5,000
-Repatriation of mortal remains	Unlimited	X
-Premature return (death of close relative)	Economy ticket	X
-Visit of close relative	Economy ticket	X
-Cost of first aid & rescue	20,000	X
-Personal liability	1,000,000	100,000
-Legal assistance & cause of redress	4,000	X
-Advance of Bail Bond (Refundable)	10,000	X
-Cancellation of Curtailment	5,000	X
-Delayed departure after12 hours	up to 500	up to 500
-Delayed baggage	250	X
-Personal baggage & money	5,000	2,000
-Loss of passport	500	350
-Personal accident	27,500	27,500
-Terrorism extension (optional)	100,000	X

Conclusion

Hospitals in Canada can charge thousands of dollars on overnight stays. Besides a plethora of expenses to be incurred if we unfortunately fall sick in between the gestation period of Provincial Health coverage. There is therefore little point in risking traveling to Canada without first getting a Canadian Travel Health Insurance Plan. The premiums are not overbearing, but the consequences can.

REFERENCES:

1. Canadian Healthcare Overview: http://www.canadavisa.com/canada-immigration-discussion-board/-t37039.0.html
2. Settlement.org

Advice: http://www.settlement.org/sys/faqs_detail.asp?k=HEALTHINS_NOOHIP&faq_id=4001251

3. US Govt. Travel
Advice: http://travel.state.gov/travel/cis_pa_tw/cis/cis_1470.html

4. Travel Ins. Quotes: http://www.travelinsurancequotes.ca/visitors-to-canada.html

5. Hepatitis-B Costs: http://www.pulsus.com/cddw2003/abs/abs170.htm

How to bring Cars into Canada?

Firstly, it is not wise to bring-in Cars from any other country into Canada. Why? Cars are quite competitively priced in Canada. It's only its maintenance & the cost of Gas that'll kill you. Secondly, Canadian models are made specifically to withstand the 'extreme' cold conditions there. Our imported cars might not [less the ones from European or similar countries].

Thirdly, there are laws for Tire, Radiator etc. modifications, before we can register it in Canada. Why would we like to take that trouble? Fourthly, the transportation costs? It might just not be worth to bring-in cars from far-flung countries.

Import Cars From The Us:

Yes, be free to bring your car/s from the US by all means. But 'remember', we need to first 'export' the car from the US and again 'import' it into Canada, after we get in. Documentations... documentations... However, quite a good detail about it is provided in this website:

http://www.auto-broker-magic.com/Canada_Import.html

Items to carry from Homeland

Very debatable... I would say, do your math first. Is the extra baggage cost worth the effort? Most items are readily available in Canada, also at very reasonable price.

Ditto for Indian Food & Spices [Rice, Dal, Pickles, Papad (?) etc.] And ditto for Italian [Pasta, Lasagna etc.], Japanese [Sushi, Tapanyaki, Teriyaki etc.], Tex-Mex, you name it.

Besides, many items are also not permitted entry. And there is otherwise a quality/quantity restriction as well. Check the CBSA website for those. Moreover, hiring a container full of goods? I'd say No... No. It may not be worthwhile at all.

What to Take? [Purely My Advice]:
1. Personal effects [for immediate use, No large quantities...]
2. General clothing [some warm ones also]
3. Laptop [No desktop, printer, etc.]
4. Digital Camcorder
5. Heirlooms [heritage collections, murals, artifacts etc.] -Check CBSA rules.
6. Original Certificates / Documents
7. Prescription Medicines
8. Books & DVDs
9. Mobile Phone* [non CDMA] -a NA charger will be needed
*Only GSM850-1900MHz models [that's the Canadian frequency -not all countries have that]

What "Not" To Take? [Purely My Advice]:
1. Furniture [whatever, small or big]
2. TV [even if it's an LCD], Fridge, Washing machine etc.
3. Curtains, Bedspreads, Pillows & linens
4. Cars, Bikes etc.
5. Large-sized Toys of kids
6. Food [Perishable or Non-perishable] items
7. Over-the-Counter Medicines
8. Meat or Meat products [including Fowl, Fish etc.]

NOTE: Asian make electronic/electrical items won't work in Canada. [Read 230 vs. 110 Volts]

Goods Lists [FORM B4 / B4A]

All goods that we carry, either 'on person' or 'following' needs to be 'listed' in form B4 / B4A, separately. These forms are available in the CBSA website, link given below:
http://www.cbsa.gc.ca/publications/forms-formulaires/b4-eng.pdf

This is the same form for 'Goods Accompanying' & 'Goods to follow'. We should club similar items in groups [e.g. DVDs: Qty-98, Books: Qty-42 etc.].

The entire list should be priced against each group & totaled in the end. We should carry 'original' invoices for high-end items [Diamonds -MUST]. Others can be broadly/generally priced, but appropriate.

Jewelry items MUST be listed [each item wise]; and should carry their "photographs". We should print-out the pictures under similar groups [e.g. Rings - all in one or more pages, Necklaces -in another page etc.]

We'll need 2 copies of each form, as one would be kept by the CBSA & one would be returned to us, for 'customs' clearance. This 2nd copy will be signed & stamped by the CBSA at the POE.

NOTE: All goods brought for 'landing' are non-taxed. If we were to bring-in goods 'later', either by personal carriage or thru a transporter, this list MUST be stamped on the 1st Landing. Else, they will be 'dutiable'. No compromise on that is possible. That's the law.

Kid's Schooling

Canada has 2 types of schools -the 'Public Schools' & the 'Catholic Schools'. There are some 'ethnic' schools as well, but not for regular education. Most of our kids [say 70%] go to the Public Schools -this education is FREE. The Catholic Schools are Fee-Paid [payable by us].

Usually, our kids will be accepted immediately into the neighborhood school, whether we arrive mid-term or during a new session. There can be an 'entry test', but that's not for rejection -but for assessment of the extra care that the school need to provide to a kid.

Even if our kids are not very good in either of the 2 Canadian official languages - English &/or French, by law a school is required to provide admission to our kids.

Each neighborhood will have their own Public School/s; and our kids are required to ONLY be admitted there. We have no choice on that. The only way out [if we think that a particular school is better] is to move our residence to that area [neighborhood]. We have to provide our 'residency contract' for this purpose.

School Websites:
Each province [& some cities] has its own 'school District Board'. All information can be viewed in those websites.
1) An example is the 'Toronto Dist. School Board', check this link:
http://www.tdsb.on.ca/
2) To see a 'ranking' overview of Canadian schools, you may like to check the following link:
http://www.fraserinstitute.org/reportcards/schoolperformance/

NOTE: Do not be hooked by the thought that the Catholic Schools are better than the Public Schools. Both are equally competitive in Education. In fact some of the Public Schools are 'excellent' & remember, 70% Canadian kids study in them.

Job Opportunities

Canada is a large country and job opportunities are different for several reasons and you do not have the same chance of getting the job you want everywhere.

• Each region has job opportunities based on the geography of that area. For example, jobs in forestry, mining and manufacturing are available in different regions of Canada.
• Jobs are also affected by changes in the economy.
• The demand for workers in some occupations and trades, such as farming, fishing and construction, is affected by the season of the year.

Where can you find information and advice on how to find a job?

Human Resources Centers of Canada (HRCC), which specialize in helping people find jobs, can provide you with helpful information. Look in your telephone directory's blue pages for the HRCC or the federal Information Centre in your area. Also, your immigrant- serving agency can help you.

HRCC counselors and staff may be able to help in several ways:

• tell you about job and language training, and work creation programs for newcomers;
• give you information to plan your job search, tell you where to have your documents translated or where to get help preparing a resume; and
• give you names of immigrant-serving agencies that might have more information.

Each HRCC has a computerized job bank that lists available jobs by occupation or profession, and by location. Read the job descriptions carefully and make sure your application clearly shows your ability to do the work.

Where else are jobs listed?

Look in the classified advertisements section of daily newspapers. Jobs are advertised according to trade, profession or service industry. Another section called 'Careers' advertises professional or managerial jobs.

The business pages of the newspaper often have information on the local economy and job market.

In many areas, there are weekly or monthly employment papers which advertise jobs. These papers are usually free and are available at many locations.

Employment agencies that hire temporary or contract staff are listed in the Yellow Pages of the telephone directory. You do not have to pay an agency or a company when you are looking for a job. The company that uses your services will pay the agency.

Are there informal sources of information about jobs?

One of the best ways to learn about jobs is to talk to people, either individuals you already know or contacts you have made through trade or professional groups, clubs or associations in your community.

This group of people is called your 'network'. Even if they cannot help you find a job, they can provide you with information, suggestions and names of people to call, as well as support and encouragement.

Should you have a resume?

Yes. Most employers want a list of your skills, education or training, and work and volunteer experience. The resume should be one to three pages, typed, and error-free.

Several sources of help are available if you need it. Job- finding clubs, HRCC counselors and reception houses may be able to help at no cost. You can buy self-help books or borrow them from a library. For a fee, a company or individual who specializes in writing resumes will help you write one.

What documents do you need to get a job in Canada?

Take most, or all, of the following documents to any job interview. Never leave behind or mail original documents. Photocopies are accepted.

Documents brought with you to Canada:

- passport, birth certificate;
- educational diplomas, degrees and certificates;
- trade or professional certifications, qualifications; and
- letters of recommendation (preferably in English or French).

Documents obtained in Canada:

- Record of Landing (visa);
- Social Insurance Number; and
- Where necessary, professional English or French translations of documents, letters and/or recommendations which may be confusing in another language.

Will you find the job you want quickly?

If you practiced a profession or trade in your country of origin, you may need to upgrade your skills to meet Canadian requirements. Your qualifications may not be accepted until you have Canadian documents or training, some work experience and good ability in English or French. Until then, you may have to accept another job.

What steps should you take to find a job?

1. Describe, in realistic terms: (a) the job(s) you want; and (b) the job(s) you would accept while looking for something better.

2. Collect all the documents you might need:

- diplomas, degrees, certificates and other qualifications;
- letters of recommendation;
- Social Insurance Number (SIN); and
- driver's license (if necessary).

3. Write a resume of your education, work and volunteer experience, skills and qualifications.

4. Learn about the labor market in your area.

5. Start and expand a network of people who might be able to direct you toward a job.

6. Check and follow up on advertisements, want ads and jobs posted in Human Resources Centers of Canada.

7. Attend interviews.

8. Telephone or write back after interviews.

9. Look for as many jobs as you can rather than wait for a particular job to come

up.

10. Keep your hopes up and look for support as you continue trying. Finding a job requires hard work and persistence.

What else should you do?

• Improve your English and/or French.
• Gain Canadian work experience even if it is not in your trade, skill or profession.
• Improve your job skills and Canadian credentials. Doing volunteer work may help.
• Understand that your first job in Canada may be the first step toward a better job.

Typically the job hunting in Canada starts with following stages:

Stage-1: 'Survival Jobs':
The moment we land [whatever city we chose], we must catch-on any opportunity that may arrive. At this stage, we must importantly keep our Ego at home. The idea is to safeguard the 'landing funds' and plan our regular expenses on any vocation based earnings. At this stage, it'll be potent to be frugal. Cut costs at all angles & get our daily meals thru whatever job that we can take. This is the most important phase of our newcomer life in Canada. If we can plan it well, we'll avoid the 'josh story', else depression shall set-in. In this phase, I might be an IT professional, an Engineer, a Doctor, whatever, or of any age bracket. I'd do well to take a job as a FedEx Helper, D2D Salesman, MacDonald Teamer, Night Watchman, Office Boy etc.
Stage Criteria: Whatever our homeland profession is, take any job to start earning.
Remember: Till now no one knows us & no one is bothered about us.
Job Search: No further search, till we get settled in this present vocation.
Timeframe: 0-3 months.

Stage-2: 'Tertiary Jobs':
Now we are fairy aware of the city & the Canadian concepts. This is the time to foray into our 2nd job. Start searching, but remember that it'll not be an actual 'job hunting' yet. In this phase, due to our awareness, we might land into an Ok job, which will be better than the survival stage. But we are still not into our choice occupation. Again it should be taken as a challenge & pursue a job that will increase our earnings from the previous one. We may not yet be satisfied with what we are doing, but shall start some savings hereon. That'll get reflected in our bank a/cs. We are actually now building our credit history, an important thing that'll hold us in good stead later. Some of the Tertiary Jobs can be Office Assistant, Hypermarket

Cashier/Teller, Warehouse Assistant, Industrial Labor Controller, Store Keeper, Security Officer/Supervisor, Courier Deliveryman etc. All of these being higher paid than minimum wage.

Stage Criteria: Try & get a better paid job than the previous one. This is applicable to any field. And complete all PR documentation.

Remember: We are still in our nascent stage. No one yet cares about us.

Job Search: Yes, keep looking at classifieds, Online, HR Agents, Networking, and Prospective Employer visits etc.

Timeframe: 3-6 months.

Stage-3: 'Intermediate Jobs':

By now we have smartened up. We are no more a novice. We have developed our links. Bank position is OK. Probably, the 'landing funds' is still not fully depleted. Our networking & friend circle has started paying. Thus, hereon we shall, most likely, get our 'first satisfactory job'. This job will be something in our related field. No, not yet what we actually have been doing in our homeland, but in the same department. The idea is to land a job within our specialty field. E.g. if I'm an IT professional, I'll get a job in the IT dept. of a company, as a first-level operator or a team leader (if I'm lucky). If I'm an Engineer, I'll be landing the job of a technician in the engineering dept. of a company. If I'm an Accountant, I'll catch hold of an Asst. Bookkeeper's task, or a financial data entry operator, or a departmental assistant. The combinations can be many. The requirement is, now start building your career. Opportunities shall commence from here onwards.

Stage Criteria: Land a job in your related field. The designation be anything, be much lower -but must be taken.

Remember: People will start knowing us in our field & thus professional growth is imminent.

Job Search: Full-fledged 'job hunting'. This hunting now is in our choice occupation.

Timeframe: 6-12 months.

Friends, hereafter we will most likely, be in our selected field of work. And we'll be aware of the job market within our profession. Hereon, we'll know what to look for & where to look for. Thus, can apply for jobs smartly & keep growing satisfactorily. It is expected that after a year at Canada, we should be able to establish ourselves nicely. Be professionally motivated and quite possibly grow well into our Canadian settlement process.

Job hunting obviously will continue until we are self-satisfied. But man we have arrived. & arrived well! In a couple of years we'll be sailing in our Original Position that we left in our homeland. And remember, we'd be still earning better than before, even if the routine costs are higher in Canada. Our margins will be much higher too. Unless we really goof-up, in 2-3 yrs. time we'll be calling the shots.

A thing to remember is that, since our 2nd stage, we should start developing our skills, by way of gaining qualifications/certifications to enhance our selected profession. As most occupations like IT, Accounts, Engineering etc. will not get us a job of that field, unless we have a Canadian Recognized Certificate. The only exception is of Doctors, who might face tremendous difficulty due to the 4 yrs. requirement of Canadian Medical studies.

The above 3 phases is also important to gain a Canadian Experience. Something we cannot do without if we want to succeed in our professions. The previous jobs can be anything, but when we try to apply for a job in our field the employers will always ask/look for a Canadian Experience. They wouldn't bother what we did, but will want an "employer's reference". This is to see our employability & people management skills. And we can't blame them as well, 'coz they need to doubly ensure that who they are employing is of 'good standing', as they have no clue of our occupations/designations in our homeland. It reminds me to advice, to do well in those previous Canadian jobs, since we'll need those employer's references, whether in writing (best to take) or telephonically by the next employer.

Note that in some cases the 1st & 2nd stages may be interlinked. Some may get promoted within the 1st stage itself & thus avoid/require a separate 2nd stage. While there are also many situations/actual cases where some PRs have settled-down well in their Tertiary Occupations itself. There is this case of an Electrical Engineer, who carried-on with his Warehouse Supervisor's job and settled down as businessman of 'Custom Bonded Warehouses' forever. There are scores of other examples.

I hope the foregoing shall lead to a proper understanding of our job-worth, & our aspirations in Canada. And help us to get hold of ourselves in a timeframe wise & market scenario wise assimilation of what, when and how to settle ourselves in this new found homeland.

Volunteer Opportunities

It is estimated that in Canada, some 12 million volunteers give their time to 161,000 charitable organizations, which generate $112 billion a year for our economy. So, there's plenty of choice to suit your needs and talents. You just have to decide what will work best for you.

Here are three questions that can help you decide:

1. What do you want back, in exchange for your time and effort? Why do you want to volunteer? Remember it's perfectly acceptable to think about gaining as a volunteer, as well as giving.

2. What do you have to offer an organization? What transferable skills, professional competences and personal qualities can you put to good use? For example, are you good at organizing and planning? Are you artistic or technically minded? Good at working in a team? Do you enjoy research and data analysis? Are you great at problem solving or strategic thinking? Are you empathetic? Can you offer practical resources, like transportation?

3. What kind of volunteer role would be a good fit for you and your lifestyle? What are you able to commit to? Be realistic. What will you do for free? How many hours do you have to spare? What else is important to you? You might consider:

   a) Distance / Travelling / Indoors / Outdoors
   b) Working alone or in a team
   c) Working with projects, animals or people (i.e., children, youth, adults, able bodied, those with disabilities, etc.)
   d) Telephone, computer or face-to-face work
   e) Local community support or international issues

If you identify an unmet need in your community, maybe you could start up a new voluntary program. The possibilities are infinite.

More tips

Here are a few tips on getting the most out of your volunteer experience:

a) Treat the voluntary work as if it's a paid job. People will be relying on you to fulfill your commitment.
b) Be responsible for your actions and decisions.
c) Be flexible and patient — your role may change at short notice; resources may be scarce.
d) Ask for references and/or testimonials from your supervisor, after an appropriate time commitment. You can use these in your job search for paid work.
e) And lastly ... enjoy yourself!

Foreign Qualified' Engineers in Canada
(Some concrete Steps to make you Street Smart)

Barriers to foreign entry are common among the Regulated Professions in Canada like Medicine, Law, Finance & Accounts, Engineering etc. This is a fact of our life & cannot be avoided... not until some drastic policy changes happen. Governmental intervention plans are many in place, but till today the market doesn't reflect any better.

Foreign-trained Engineers, who arrive in Canada with high hopes, only to have their careers derailed, have genuine reasons to crib. Ms. Marie Lemay, CEO of the CCPE (Canadian Council of Professional Engineers) said that, foreign-trained engineers have been caught in a Catch-22 situation, unable to find permanent employment because they had no domestic work experience and unable to get that experience because their degrees had no currency with Canadian employers.

The situation is:
"To get that work experience, you have to get a job, but to get the job you have to either have that work experience OR employers value your credentials [degrees & experience], which is not forthcoming". This is a Catch-22, you bet!

Startling Facts : Under-Utilization of Engineers
• Yearly engineering supply from all sources has grown by a factor of three, and immigration into the engineering profession has increased by a factor of twelve, in a decade in which net jobs and economic growth in Canada has been less than 20%
• More than 75% of all skilled workers immigrating to Canada who intend to work in a regulated profession are engineers: this includes the total of all doctors, lawyers, teachers, nurses, veterinarians, optometrists, accountants...
• A popular trend shows immigrant engineers, though well qualified, but is excluded from the workforce because his credentials are not recognized.
• Some senior engineers and engineering educators consider engineering to be the "new liberal arts education", and have no expectation that engineering graduates should have the opportunity to work as engineers if they so choose! This attitude is not marginal- it is surprisingly widespread!
• Recent surveys have indicated that a large fraction of working engineers considers themselves to be "overqualified for the work they do"; and that about 75% of professional engineers have no defined area of work. A large fraction of engineers are not engaged in the practice of engineering as conventionally defined.
• We still hear reports of localized shortages of engineers. Why? Because some firms insist on hiring people with Canadian experience to fill certain positions that is

actually entry level. And other firms wouldn't hire at the entry level with foreign-qualified engineers.

Concrete Steps we should take to Combat the above
• If you are a new immigrant, first & foremost get your 'foreign' credentials assessed within Canada (details below [1]).
• Secondly, obtain memberships / certifications of Canadian bodies / institutes / associations (details below [2]).
• Thirdly, get yourselves re-trained from Canadian Universities / Institutions. Most, if not all universities have engineering faculties.
• Fourthly, by the time you endorse into an engineering degree program, get that certification, for sure, as mentioned in point-2 above.
• Fifthly, if you are a recent graduate of an engineering program, or you have an 'overseas engineering education and have been unable to find suitable work as an engineer, contact your university, accreditation body, professional licensing body, and let them 'know' that you exist! Network & gather all your colleagues, peers, friends, who are in the same situation and write/approach 'jointly' to these bodies for assistance!

[1] Engineering International- Education Assessment Program
While it is not part of licensing, the Engineering International-Education Assessment Program assesses the educational qualifications of individuals who were educated and trained outside of Canada by comparing their education to a Canadian engineering education. The assessment provides applicants with valuable information on how their foreign education compares to a Canadian engineering education. Few of the agencies to approach are:

1. Canadian Council of Professional Engineers (CCPE)
http://www.engineerscanada.ca/e/pr_international_ieg_3.cfm
2. Canadian Engineering Accreditation Board (CEAB)
http://www.accreditation.org/accbodies.php?page=canada

[2] Memberships / Certifications from Engineering Bodies
Similar to a driver's permit, the memberships/certifications, will instantly qualify immigrants to work in an "apprenticeship capacity" as they pursue their supplementary training [Canadian re-training] toward a permanent placement. Some of the organizations you can approach are:

1. Professional Engineers Ontario licenses [PEO]
http://www.peo.on.ca/
2. The Council for Access to the Profession of Engineering [CAPE]
http://capeinfo.ca/

3. Association of Professional Engineers, Geologists & Geophysicists of Alberta [APEGGA]
http://www.apegga.org/applicants/ieg/overview.html

REFERENCE READING:
Barriers to 'Foreign Trained' Engineers...
http://www.geography.ryerson.ca/hbauder/Immigrant%20Labour/immigrant_credentials.pdf

The Medical Practitioner's Road Map
(A brief scenario of what to Expect & what To Do -to succeed in Canada)

Only one-quarter of immigrants educated outside Canada are working in medical, law and teaching occupations for which they're trained, according to a report from Statistics Canada. And with Doctors the problem seems to be an everlasting one.

Foreign-trained doctors who immigrate to Canada face a rigorous licensing process in which they must prove themselves worthy of a residency seat in the Canadian medical system. But many -often despite 7-10+ yrs. of experience, hit a serious roadblock when it comes to qualifying & becoming a medical practitioner in Canada.

What the Bosses say?

"I am told there are at least a thousand doctors from different jurisdictions that are in Canada that aren't practicing," said Dosanjh. "We need to re-skill them, retrain them and bring them on stream so they can do what they do best instead of driving cabs".
-Ujjal Dosanjh, Federal Health Minister, Sep. 27 2004

"Alberta doesn't have a doctor shortage, but a shortage of practicing doctors. We have a huge talent pool that will stale date if we don't get immigrant physicians into medical practice".
-Dr. David Watt, University of Calgary language education researcher

"We have people who have been the heads of emergency medicine in hospitals servicing a population of a million, anesthetists who have been practicing for 20 years. After they pass all the exams, go through all the hoops, they can't even mop a floor in a hospital let alone work as a medical professional".
-Dr. Patrick Coady, Association of International Medical Doctors of British Columbia

The Procedure to become 'Practicing Doctors' in Canada:
In simple terms, an expatriate doctor must get Retrained, pass some Exams, complete a 1 yr. Internship then apply for a 2 yr. Residency Position. The total Timeframe in theory should take 4-5 yrs., before being 'permitted' to practice medicine. But is it? Here are the Steps involved:

Step-1: Language Tests (Written & Oral):
All foreign-trained doctors firstly, must pass the language tests [2 types -written as well as oral] to practice in this country.

Step-2: Canadian Medical Course & Exam:

Secondly, doctors must take Canadian university courses and are required to sit for a series of exams. These are two [2] exams -one written and one clinical - administered by the Ontario International Medical Graduate Program [similar in other provinces].These are the Qualifying Exams before they are allowed to practice medicine.

Step-3: Medical Practice of 1 year:

In order to be accepted into Residency Programs, they must have at least one [1] year of continuous medical practice within the previous four years. This is usually a hands-on training under a qualified medical practitioner.

Step-4: The Residency Program of 2 years:

The last step is to apply for a two [2] year residency position under the Canadian Resident Matching Service (CaRMS) which are administered by universities and hospitals together.

Step-5: Medical Council of Canada's Evaluation Exam:

As a final step, there is the Medical Council of Canada's Evaluation Exam, which all foreign doctors must write to obtain his Medical License. And thereon, s/he can practice medicine in Canada.

So, where is the Problem?

The foregoing 5 steps seem to be fairly Ok. Though time consuming, but is achievable, Right? **Wrong**... there is a problem.

Problem-1: Govt. Policy - say Apathy:

Canada's doctor shortage is partly rooted in a 1991 report commissioned by the provincial deputy ministers of health. In that document, Morris Barer and Greg Stoddart, two health economists, predicted that Canada was facing a physician surplus. In response, provincial governments, scrambling to save money, cut first-year enrollment to Canadian medical schools by about ten percent.

Thus, however smart & experienced an overseas qualified a doctor is, the openings in those provincial medical schools / colleges are not enough. There is stiff competition, assessment tests & accessibility of a fair passage. Thus, getting pass those is a behemoth task for an expatriate doctor.

Problem-2: Scarcity of Residency Openings:

A major problem is the shortage of residency openings. An American residency is treated on a par with a Canadian one, but doctors from other countries are not.

Therefore, the majority of immigrant doctors have to complete a residency here. "The snag is getting the residency, you can pass all your exams, but you still can't get into a training program."

Foreign doctors can compete with Canadian medical school graduates for residency positions. But there is a catch: Foreign doctors will only be considered after Canadian-trained graduates have found residency positions. They can compete in the second round -for the leftovers. The competition is stiff. In 2003, 625 international graduates competed. Only 67 -about ten percent, found a position.

In every province the situation regarding residency positions varies: the number of positions available, the rules about how to get them and how long a doctor has to train. Each province sets aside a few positions for foreign doctors, but in no province is the number of residencies available equal to the number of doctors seeking to fill them.

Problem-3: Qualifying for the Residency Programs:
Foreign-trained doctors are caught in a Catch-22. In order to be accepted into residency programs, they must have at least one year of continuous medical practice. This is nearly impossible to accomplish. 'Coz, upon immigrating to Canada, doctors also must take Canadian university courses and are required to sit for provincial and federal exams before they are allowed to practice medicine. There lies the problem: they cannot get the residency without the experience and cannot practice in Canada without passing the qualifying exams, a complex situation, albeit.

Problem-4: Time, Effort & Money:
This education, examination, training & residency process can be lengthy and costs quite a lot. Most of us have dug into all our savings & 'landed' here. How many of us can afford long standing retraining costs, besides devoting some serious time over our family responsibilities? And if all goes well it would yet take 4-5 years to complete. But, if we run into red-flags, the timeframe can be anything. How many of us would have that perseverance?

Some Examples:

(a) In Iran, Dr. Shahab Khanahmad had worked as a family physician for two years. He also worked as an assistant in the Teheran University Neurology Dept.'s clinical Electrophysiology Lab, studying diseases such as Epilepsy. But in Canada, Khanahmadi hasn't been able to work as a doctor. The closest he's come to a hospital is as an unpaid assistant to a Neurologist and as a Volunteer in a family practice. The 32-year-old says, "I am so disappointed."

Dr. Khanahmadi came to Vancouver in September 2001. He studied in UBC, passed all Canadian medical exams and in 2004 applied for a residency position under the CaRMS. He got two interviews but no position. That year British Columbia had only six positions set aside in family practice for immigrant doctors. After 2 more year's attempts, in 2007 he finally got his residential opening.

(b) Dr. Bashir started studying medicine ab-initio in Canada. After 3 yrs. of medical school & clearing the qualifying exams he needed to pass the clinical exam. Bashir says, "I had never failed an exam in my life." But the first time he took the Ontario exams, his clinical scores were not high enough to be accepted into the program. He tried again a year later, with the same disappointing result.

When he wasn't on social assistance, Bashir worked as a cabbie and a dishwasher. He tried the exams again in 2002 and 2003. His written results were always among the highest out of some 500 candidates. But the examiners weren't satisfied with his clinical skills. They told Bashir his accent made it difficult for patients to understand him [though he had passed the Language Exams].

Finally, in 2004, almost 9 years and 15 exams later, Bashir got closer to practicing here as a doctor. He secured a residency at McMaster. It was what he had always wanted, but he says, "I am 33. I've lost nine years -almost a third of my life."

Solution to the Problem:
"Admitting qualified doctors makes economic sense. If a foreign-trained doctor requires additional training to come up to Canadian standards, it is far cheaper to provide it than to educate a doctor entirely from scratch". *Herb Emery*, an associate professor of economics at the University of Calgary says. "It costs Alberta taxpayers about $300,000 to put a student through 3 years of medical school. This would be saved if immigrants who already have medical degrees were accepted for residencies'.

Currently, there is news of 250 foreign-trained doctors who chose to settle in Quebec, where thousands of inhabitants are in need of a family doctor. These doctors have passed national licensing examinations. They have passed provincial licensing examinations. They have passed language proficiency tests. But they aren't practicing today. We should be asking why?

Dr. Albert Schumacher, president of the medical association, said retraining international doctors isn't quite that easy. There are about 1,000 individuals who are qualified to do residency training, but they've had little or no experience working with actual patients. He says, "Getting immigrant doctors into the system would be a good idea but it's the fast-track that becomes difficult."

"Not only did they cut back our medical school numbers but they also cut back resident medical training spots and those spots went up in vapor too," he adds. The only quick solution would be for the federal government to pay for extra residency spots in Canada's medical schools, he said.

Conclusion:
Before medical doctors can practice in any Canadian province, they must complete a residency program, which is a paid hospital position considered the last step in medical training. This applies to doctors trained in Canada and doctors educated abroad. But there is an important difference between these two groups: nearly all Canadian medical school graduates are accepted into residency positions, but only just over a quarter of foreign-trained doctors were able to find a residency position last year. **How could this be?**

They are the victims of a complicated bureaucracy that seems intent on shutting out foreign-trained physicians. But, that's not going to remain true. There is a silver line visible beyond the dark clouds.

The AIPSO proposal is under study [link below]. And Govt. is seriously thinking of implementing it in its entirety. And there are success stories too, which should be a morale booster to many 'landed' doctors -read the stories of Dr. Saldhana & Dr. Nirvair Kaur [link below].

REFERENCES:
1) The AIPSO Proposal
http://www.aipso.ca/pages/docs/romanow%20submission%20final%20version.htm
2) The Doctors' Dilemma
http://www.buzzle.com/articles/canadian-dilemma-doctors-who-flip-hamburgers.html
3) Conspiracy Theories
http://www.cbc.ca/whitecoat/2008/05/conspiracy_theories_on_canadas.html
4) David Cohen's Article
http://www.canadavisa.com/canada-immigration-blog/2007/05/game-is-rigged.html
5) Minister Ujjal Dosanjh asserts
http://www.ctv.ca/servlet/ArticleNews/story/CTVNews/1096331488269_10
6) Why is Canada Shutting Out Doctors
http://www.readersdigest.ca/mag/2004/08/doctors.html

Success Stories:
7) Dr. Colin Saldanha
http://www.canadianimmigrant.ca/immigrantstories/health/article/767
9) Dr. Nirvair Kaur Levitt
http://www.canadianimmigrant.ca/immigrantstories/health/article/548

Self-Created Jobs

HOW CAN I CREATE MY OWN JOB?

EnterWeb
http://www.enterweb.org
A Canadian site, EnterWeb is an Internet Virtual Library with an international perspective. It has information on all aspects of entrepreneurship, self-employment, and small business management. The site is organized into broad topics, such as international commerce, economic development, financing, small business management, e-commerce and many others. This is a very complete site.

EntreWorld
http://www.EntreWorld.org
Possibly the most impressive of all information sources on entrepreneurship! This site is jam-packed with articles, tools, and advice on all issues related to setting up your own business. Start-up difficulties, balancing business and family life, planning for growth - these questions and more are addressed here!

(CIP) If you are thinking of starting your own business or becoming self-employed, read the articles in the "Entrepreneurship as a career" section. See:
http://www.EntreWorld.org/Content/SYB.cfm?Topic=YouECarr
This should give you plenty to think about!

Canada Business Services Centers (CBSC)
http://www.cbsc.org/main.html
The CBSC's mission is to provide start-up assistance to new entrepreneurs, to help small business and to encourage entrepreneurial growth. No matter what field you are interested in, this site will provide vital information on governmental assistance programs. Peruse the directory or use the search engine to find the information you need more quickly. You will find a link to your province's CBSC web site on the home page, where you can find even more information.

(CIP) When writing your business plan, use the Interactive Business Planner at:
http://www.cbsc.org/ibp

Some tools

Intervision -Youth Business Online (Canadian Youth Business Foundation)
http://www.cybf.ca
The Canadian Youth Business Foundation offers technical advice and support to young entrepreneurs. This site provides a number of tools to help you with your start-up: different models of a business plan, a directory of available financing, a guide to business regulations, and a listing of advisors and experts in many provinces. There is even a newsgroup for young entrepreneurs and an online counseling service, as well as a description of the Foundation's own financing and mentoring programs.

Online Small Business Workshop
http://www.cbsc.org/osbw/workshop.html
This site is a must! Produced by the CBSC British Columbia, this is a truly complete guide to founding a small business. It deals with everything from the original business idea to the actual start-up, from financing to planning to marketing. Each section is full of precious advice and information. Its comprehensiveness will astound you!

Tip: To fully benefit from the information presented on this site, go through each section in order. Don't just browse through it.

(CIP) The section on business idea is a gem. Check it out at:
http://www.cbsc.org/osbw/concepts.html

Strategies- Business Support and Financing
http://strategis.ic.gc.ca/sc_mangb/engdoc/homepage.html
Home page- http://strategis.ic.gc.ca
Both the would-be entrepreneur and the seasoned business owner will appreciate the wealth of information on business tools and resources, financing for growth, international marketing, e-commerce, government programs, and other important issues published on this site. In fact, you can probably find any business information that you may need on this site alone!

Strategies - Starting a Small Business
http://strategis.ic.gc.ca/SSG/mi05I72e.html
Home page: http://strategis.ic.gc.ca
Eager to start your business, but don't know how to deal with legalities? Need to understand the law better? Click on the "Business Roadmaps' for a quick guide by province. Learn about registering your business, licenses, taxation rules,

employment standards, and other important matters. This site offers informative articles, a software directory, and a listing of agencies that will help you get started off on the right foot. Very useful!

Tip: To gain the knowledge you need to, participate effectively in the global economy, click on "Multi-cultural Advisors" to find people and organizations that will help you to do business equally well at home or abroad.

Business Development Bank of Canada
http://www.bdc.ca
The Business Development Bank of Canada (BDC) is Canada's small business bank. You will find a description of its financial programs under various headings; business start-up, business growth, exporting, refinancing, etc. You will also find links to many other sites with relevant services or information. The BDC also offers consulting and management services. To find the BDC's office in your area, select your province from the "Your Local Connection" field.

For the Aspiring Entrepreneur

Paul and Sarah Edwards Web Site

http.//www.paulandsarah.com/indeX.asp

Paul and Sarah Edwards are well-known authors and experts on self- employment. They offer advice to entrepreneurs such as start-up ideas, marketing tips, and much more. A worthwhile site!

(CIP) Looking for a start-up idea for your own business? You will find 1600 of them at:

http://www.paulandsarah.com/Pages/perfwork/frame1600perf.html

Minding Your Own Business

http://www.hrdc-drhc.gc.ca/career-carriere/minding/mind-eng/index.shtml Home page: http://www.hrdc-drhc.gc.ca/career-carriere

Do you want to start your own business but are not sure what it involves? Or if you have what it takes? This site can address some of your doubts. It will help you understand the personal qualities and skills that you will need to run your own business. It outlines the different types of business structures and approaches that you will need to consider. The experiences of other entrepreneurs illustrate each section and there are links to other resources.

Calmeadow

http://www.calmeadow.com

Calmeadow is a Canadian, non-profit organization dedicated to helping the self-employed access credit and financing. It also offers micro-financing. Small loans are offered to groups of people who are setting up their own micro-business. These peer groups provide support, collaboration, and shared accountability. This site explains in detail the procedures involved in setting up a peer group and lists a number of other micro-financing services across Canada.

Self-Employment Development Initiatives (SEDI)

http://www.sedi.org/1index.html

This web site will introduce you to the Self Employment Assistance Program (SEAP) that enables unemployed people to start their own micro-business while receiving Employment Insurance benefits. Note that this is an HRDC program and is available elsewhere in Canada, even though this site offers information that is specific to Toronto.

Canadian Tax Guide for New Immigrants can be found on the below link, it will answer your most of the queries.

http://www.cra-arc.gc.ca/tx/nnrsdnts/ndvdls/nwcmr-eng.html

The below link about the tax treaties is useful.

http://www.cra-arc.gc.ca/tx/nnrsdnts/trty-eng.html

Missing out on tuition help?

Six years after the launch of the Canada Learning Bond, the families of only 212,000 children, or 19 per cent of those eligible, have taken advantage of the benefit.

Only one in five low-income families in Canada has taken up the federal government's offer of free money for their children's post-secondary education, shows a study released in December by Toronto's Omega Foundation.

Six years after the launch of the Canada Learning Bond, the families of only 212,000 children, or 19 per cent of those eligible, have taken advantage of the benefit. Through the learning bond, Ottawa contributes a maximum of $2,000 to a low-income child's tax-sheltered registered education savings plan (RESP).

Yet as of 2009, more than 880,000 children had not claimed the bond they were entitled to.
"The federal program is benefiting the high-income families, when the low-income families can benefit from it most," said May Wong, Omega's executive director and a report co-author. "The money can make a big difference in their children's academic aspirations."

To receive the learning bond, families have to have a child born Jan. 1, 2004, or after, and an after-tax household income under $40,970 a year. Then, it is necessary to start an RESP account with a licensed RESP provider where the government can deposit the money. Parents and child also need to have a social insurance number.

A previous survey, published in 2008 by EKOS, showed that only one in 10 low-income families had heard of the free learning bond and only 83 per cent had heard of RESPs in general.

The report attributes this gap, especially among immigrants, to the lack of multilingual information, and to the ignorance of community workers about the RESP.

Nasrin Khatam, originally from Iran, learned about the RESP only when she was approached by a sales representative of a private scholarship fund at a mall. "He told me how much the money would grow but didn't say anything about the processing fees and investment risks," said the Toronto graphic designer, who had to pay a large penalty for stopping payments to her son's scholarship fund after being laid off in 2008.

But, overall, RESPs can be a solid investment in your children's educational future, as the federal government provides a payment of at least 20 per cent of the total annual contributions you make to the RESP, up to $2,500 per child, through something called the Canada Education Savings Grant (CESG). The CESG's lifetime limit per child is $7,200.

Find out more information on the Canada Learning Bond, RESPs and more at canlearn.ca.

Canada is rolling out new mentoring programs in various parts of the country for extending opportunities to new immigrants.

ACCES Employment Services, an immigrant employment agency in Canada, is providing a Speed Mentoring pilot program throughout the nation to help new immigrants over the common barriers to success in getting jobs in the country.

The speed mentoring program aims to enable new immigrants in Canada get connected with the employers in the nation.

ACCES is hosting a huge networking program at the Toronto Board of Trade today for beginning the 'Speed Mentoring' program.

The program aims to help around 100 new immigrants in Canada seeking jobs in the nation. In addition, around 100 managers and executives from nearly 65 companies are also likely to participate in the pilot program.

The 10-minutes speed mentoring program for newcomers in Canada will focus on giving information related to various sectors including engineering and finance, sales and marketing and IT (information technology).

Several previous studies have reiterated about the higher levels of productivity and innovation by immigrants to the Canadian firms employing them. And despite of having higher qualifications and work experience, immigrants continue to face several obstacles in getting jobs in Canada.

This is evident from the higher unemployment rate for new immigrants in Canada which is around 17 percent in the city of Toronto. This results in making far less competitive in the world.

As per the findings of a GTA study in the year 2009, immigrants with English-sounding names and having Canadian work experience were more likely to be called for an interview than applicants with foreign credentials and Indian, Chinese or Pakistani names.

Canada is facing increasing skill shortages primarily due to shrinking number of adults in the working-age. And hence, there is an increasing need for giving due recognition to the skills and credentials possessed by immigrants in Canada to help them get employment in their respective fields.

The new Speed Mentoring Program sponsored by BMO Financial Group will involve providing information and guidance related to different sectors and different occupations for the benefit of the newcomers in Canada.

Around 1,600 professional new immigrants have benefited from the Speed Mentoring program by ACCES in the last four years and the job success rate of this program at five locations throughout Canada has been around 80 percent.

How to obtain Ontario Driving License?

The procedure of obtaining a Canadian driving license is pretty much simple within our 1st few days [max a week]. Remember, this is 'easy' if we are coming from countries which have a similar driving & road management conditions [read 'left-hand drive']. If not, we may have to undertake some training before we apply.

Pre-conditions / Which License:

1. If we have over 24 months 'overseas' driving experience -we get the Ontario G2 Driving License.
2. If we have over 12 months [but less than 24] driving experience -we get the Ontario G1 Driving License.
(Details below)

Direct Swap of Licenses:

If our home country doesn't have a *reciprocal license exchange agreement with Ontario, we cannot Swap our current D/License to get a Toronto-ON D/License.
*Reciprocal License Exchange Agreement exists between Ontario and: US, Japan, Korea, Switzerland, Germany, France, UK, Austria & Belgium.

What is the Procedure then:

But, in that case do we have to START all over Again? **No**... We can immediately apply & get a Toronto (Ontario) Driving License thru the following procedure:

Step-1 -Before we 'Land':

1. We must obtain a 'Letter of Authentication'* from the country's Roads & Transport Authority, explaining** our D/License.
2. Take also a 'True Translation Copy'* of our D/License from Road & Transport Authority. Both 1 & 2 maybe clubbed in one.
3. Obtain an International Driving License/Permit*** (IDL / IDP) stating "more than 24 months" driving experience in our country.

*In English or French, the 2 Canadian Official Languages.

**The explanation should include 24 or 12 months driving experience [the Pre-conditions will apply].

***This is nothing but a translated copy of our present D/license. (It can be used in lieu of point-1 & 2 above).

Benefits of the IDL / IDP:

With the foregoing, we can drive a car abroad for three [3] months (2 months, in Ontario). Within that time apply for the Ontario Driving License. These International Driving Licenses [IDL/IDP] are issued against our original D/Licenses by the Automobile Associations or [sometimes] the RTA/RTO of our home country. Check them for more details.

Step-2 -After you 'Land':
In such cases we are called 'Out of Country Drivers' and we can skip the G2 'waiting period' and get the G2 license immediately [with that 24 months letter] or a G1 driving license [if we only have the above 12 months letter].

Now for the Ontario driver's license are required to;
1. Present a valid foreign Driver's License*,
2. Provide an acceptable Proof of Identity [SIN, PR card etc.]
3. Pay all applicable Fees,
4. Pass a Vision Test
5. Pass the Written Knowledge Test -regarding Ontario's traffic rules.
*If it is not in English or French, it is to be accompanied by a written translation from a qualified translator; [we got that, as the Authentication Letter]

Note: Applicants are required to provide adequate proof of foreign driving experience. However, if it is not there, the ministry will accept applicants' declaration of their foreign driving experience on the driver's license application for up to a maximum of 12 months experience. In that case we get the G1* license only.

Step-3 -The Tests to take:
Based on the 24 months Authentication Letter the ministry will recognize the applicant's foreign driving experience as certified on the authentication letter AND,

1. After Step-2, we can attempt the G2*Exit Road Tests (mandatory wait times are waived).
2. Upon successfully passing the G2* Exit Road Test, we get the G2* license.
3. After few months of driving under G2* we can apply for a G*License.
4. If we 'only' have the 12 months letter & not the 24, we qualify for G1* Road Test & the G1* driving license only.
5. If we don't provide any letter, we must pass the G1* road test and have a 12-month wait period for taking G2* road test.

*The License Grading Explained [G1, G2 & G]:
-G1 License has certain limitations like we have to always drive along with a G license holder. It is thus, useless for us, who have good & adequate driving experience under similar driving conditions & system as that of Canada [read 'left-hand drive' experience & similar road/traffic management conditions].
-G2 License is as good as G, except that we cannot drive on the Highway at certain times (Midnight Rush Hrs. when truck movement starts).

-G License is the 'full-fledged' driving license.

Source:
http://www.drivetest.ca/en/license/OutOfCountryDrivers.aspx

Note:
1. The above procedure is mainly addressed for the Ontario (ON) province.
2. The procedure is pretty much similar with all other provinces as well [BC, NS, NB, etc.].
3. If we are not coming from a similar driving condition country, we must take some training before we proceed.
4. Usually we can get the G2 driving license quite easily [with the foregoing steps].

APPENDIX I – Employment Agencies - General

ACE PERSONNEL SERVICES
Industrial Jobs
2421/2 Queen St. E. Toronto (at Sherbourne)
Tel: (416) 368-7773
Monday-Friday: 5am-6pm
1515 Matheson Blvd. E. #207 at Dixie Mississauga
Tel: (905) 625-1944 Monday-Friday: 9am-4pm

ADECCO
Industrial Jobs

168 Kennedy Road S. Brampton
Tel.: (905) 455-5800
Website: www.adecco.ca
611-1280 Finch Ave. W. (Keele/Finch)
Tel: (416) 661-2325 Fax: (416) 661-8203

ADVANCED WELDING TECHNIQUES INC.
Welder Training Facility

1016 Upper Wellington, Hamilton, Ontario L9A 3S3
Tel: (905) 575-8311, 1-800-794-7840

AIMCO
Industrial Jobs

96 Rexdale Blvd. Suite 201
Monday-Friday: 9am-2pm
700 Dundas St. E. Suite 10 (Dundas/Cawthra) Mississauga
Tel.: (905) 896-3181
Monday-Friday: 8am-2pm
284 Queen Street E. Unit 123 (at Hansen beside Just Desserts) Brampton
Tel.: (905) 454-4972
Monday-Friday: 8am-2pm

ALL THE WAY PERSONNEL

Industrial Jobs

964 Albion Road Suite 109 (#73 Bus from Royal York Station) (on top of No-Frills)
Tel.: (416) 744-2560

APPLEONE TEMPORARY/FULL-TIME EMPLOYMENT SERVICES
Industrial & Office Jobs

Brampton Tel.: (905) 453-8000
E-mail: inetbrampton @ mail.appleone.com
Etobicoke Tel.: (416) 236-4000
E-mail: inetetobicoke @ mail.appleone.com
Meadowvale Tel.: (905) 567-9990 E-mail: inetmeadowvale @ mail.appleone.com
Mississauga Tel.: (905) 277-2770 E-mail: inetmississauga @ mail.appleone.com
Website: www.appleone.com
Monday-Friday: 10.00am & 1.30pm

A.T.I.
Industrial Jobs

5160 Explorer Dr. Unit 38 Mississauga
(Eglinton & Renforth)
9am to 3pm

ATLAS PLACEMENT SERVICES INC.
Industrial Jobs

74 Queen Street West
(1 Block West of Hwy. 10 on North Side of Queen St.) Brampton Monday-Friday:
7am-6pm
Fax: (905) 451-9860

BRADSON STAFFING SERVICES
(See Spherton Workforce Architects, below)
Industrial & Office Jobs

253 Queen St. E. Unit 5 Brampton
Tel.; (905) 452-7169 Fax: (905) 452-7663 www.bradson.com

BURNS
Security Jobs

Tel: (416) 223-3995

CANADIAN EMPLOYMENT CONTRACTORS INC.
Industrial Jobs

1425 Dundas Street East, Suite 208 Mississauga, Ontario
Tel: (905) 282-9578 Fax: (905) 282-9582

CAN WORK CORP (CWC)
Office/Industrial Jobs

1370 Dundas Street East (Dixie/Dundas) Suite 204
(Second Floor)
Tel.: (905) 566-9734
Fax: (905) 451-7028 Tuesday, Wednesday, Thursday: at 9.30am & 3.30pm
105 Queen St. W. Brampton
Fax: (905) 451-7028
1315 Finch Ave. W. (at Keele) Suite 208

CAPP EMPLOYMENT SERVICES INC.
Permanent & Temporary Office Jobs

Tel.: (905) 625-4400 Fax: (905) 625-4433
E-mail: employ @ cappcon.com

CAREER CONNECTIONS
Office Jobs

Tel.: (905) 824-7448 Fax: (905) 824-6533
E-mail: zag.dutton @ sympatico.ca

CONTACT SOLUTIONS GROUP INC.
Telemarketing Jobs

40 Eglinton Ave E. 8th Fl.
Tel.: (416) 932-6471

CONTEMPORARY PERSONNEL INC.
Industrial Jobs

7700 Hurontario Street 2nd Floor Suite 411 Brampton
(in the City South Plaza)

Tel.: (905) 457-8970
Website: www.contemporary.ca or bramp @ contemporary.ca
Monday-Thursday: 9.30am to 12.00noon and 1.00pm to 3.30pm

COURTNEY PERSONNEL INC.
Office Jobs

Tel.: (905) 452-7762, (905) 452-9555
E-mail: courtneypers @ sprint.ca

DORVICT RESOURCE & CONSULTING CENTRE INC.
Office Jobs

3461 Dixie Road Suite 402 Mississauga, Ontario L4Y 3X4 Fax: (905) 624-7597

DYNAMIC EMPLOYMENT SOLUTIONS INC.
Office Jobs

Tel: (905) 796-3300 Fax: (905) 796-0043
Website: www.dynamicemployment.com
Emails: roxannk @ dynamicemployment.com
moniquej @ dynamicemployment.com
nickib @ dynamicemployment.com

DYNAMIC EXECUTIVE SEARCH
Office Jobs

Website: www.dynamicexecutive.ca
Emails: nwiesner @ dynamicexecutive.ca
shyndman @ dynamicexecutive.ca

ELITE TEMPORARIES
Industrial Jobs

7171 Torbram Road Unit 5 Mississauga (Derry & Torbram) Tel.: (905) 678-7494

ENDEAVOUR PERSONNEL LTD.
Office Jobs

160 Wilkinson Rd. Units 23 & 24 Brampton, Ont. L6T 4Z4
Tel.: (905) 457-3074 Fax: (905) 457-1826
1310 Dundas St. East Suite 215 Mississauga, Ont. L4Y 2C1

Tel.: (905) 272-9335 Fax: (905) 272-4276
Monday-Thursday: 8.00am to 4.00pm
Friday: 9.00am to 3.00pm

FIRM RECRUIT STAFFING
Permanent and Contract Office Jobs

60 Bristol Road East
Suite #105
Mississauga, Ontario
L4Z 3K8
Tel.: (416) 827-5833 Fax: (905) 804-8348
Email: firmrecruit @ mail.com

FIRST CHOICE PERSONNEL
Office Jobs

Tel.: (416) 241-8611 Fax: (416) 241-4152
Website: www.firstchoicepersonnel.com
E-mail: Virginia @ firstchoicepersonnel.com

GLOBAL PLACEMENT SERVICES
Industrial Jobs

7025 Tomken Road Suite 239 Mississauga,
Ontario L5S 1R6
Tel.: (905) 565-0310 Fax: (905) 565-0311
Monday-Friday: 10.00am to 3.00pm

IDEAL PERSONNEL
Office Jobs

55, City Centre Dr. (Suite 307)
Tel.: (905) 279-8050 Fax: (905) 279-0901
www.idealpersonnel.com

INTEGRA I.T. PARTNERS INC.
Information Technology Jobs

40 Eglinton Avenue East, Suite 601, Toronto,
Ontario M4P 3A2
Tel.: (416) 487-3301

E-mail: recruiting @ integrait.com

INTERIM PERSONNEL
(See Spherton Workforce Architects, below)
Office & Industrial Jobs

151 City Centre Drive Suite 502 Mississauga
Tel.: (905) 459-5285
8 Nelson St. W. (Main and Nelson) Brampton Suite 104A

INTERTEC SECURITY
Security Jobs

939 Eglinton Ave. E. (1 Block west of Leslie St.)
Tel: (416) 424-2002

JMR PERSONNEL SERVICES
Drivers & Industrial Jobs

6299 Airport Road Suite 702 Mississauga
(American Dr./Airport Rd.)

KELLY SERVICES
Industrial Jobs

20 Nelson St. W. Ste. 404 (Nelson/George St.)
50 Burnhamthorpe Rd. W. Ste. 303 (Burnhamthorpe/Hurontario)
1120 Finch Ave. W. Ste. 105 (Finch/Keele)
710 Dorval Dr. Ste. 105 (dorval/Wyecroft)
Tel: 1-888-464-5355
Website: www.kellyservices.ca

LABOUR READY TEMPORARY SERVICES LTD.
Industrial Jobs

440 Horner Avenue Etobicoke
Tel: (416) 253-4434
30 A Kennedy Rd. S. #3 Brampton
Tel: (905) 459-2666
5170 Dixie Rd. Unit 8 Mississauga
Tel: (905) 206-9442
3850 Steeles Avenue W. Woodbridge

Tel: (905) 850-2444
1-888-24-LABOUR

LAIDLAW EDUCATION SERVICES
School Bus Drivers

1100 Central Parkway West Unit 30
(Southwest corner of Central Parkway West & Erindale Station Road in Mississauga)
Tel: (905) 804-0499 1-877-914-KIDS

LOGISTICS PERSONNEL RESOURCES INC.
Industrial Jobs

680 Silver creek Blvd. #102A 2nd Floor
(Cawthra Rd. 1 Block North of Dundas St. E.)
Tel: (905) 275-0385 Fax: (905) 275-4101
Monday-Friday: 8am-2pm

MAINGATE PERSONNEL SERVICES INC.
Industrial Jobs

5340 Maingate Dr. (between Dixie & Tomken off Matheson) Tel.: (905) 625-2086

MANPOWER
Office/Industrial Jobs

2 County Court Blvd. Suite 335
Brampton: Tel.: (905) 454-3331 Fax: (905) 454-4964
1 City Centre Drive Suite 810
Mississauga:
Tel.: (905) 276-2000 Fax: (905) 276-2596
E-mail: angeline.tham @ na.manpower.com

MEADOWVALE SECURITY
Security Jobs

Tel.: (905) 821-0163 or (416) 587-6663

MILLENNIUM RECRUITING
Office Jobs

Tel: (905) 271-4378 Fax: (905) 271-4405

OLSTEN STAFFING SERVICES
Industrial Jobs

7007 Islington Avenue suite 204 (at Steels)
Tel.: (905) 850-7800
Monday-Friday: 9.00am to 5.00pm
Tel.: (905) 896-8955 Fax: (905) 896-8926
E-mail: filander.lima @ olsten.com Ollie.becks @ olsten.com

ON TIME PERSONNEL LTD.
Industrial Jobs

1185 Dundas St. E. Suite 204
(2 blocks west of Dixie at Palstan)
Tel.: (905) 848-3995
Monday-Friday: 9.00am to 5.00pm

ON THE DOUBLE (OTD)
Drivers

6605 Ordan Drive, Mississauga (Dixie Rd. & Courtney Park) Tel: (905) 565-8300
Ext. 226 1-888-812-1192

PDQ PERSONNEL INC.
Industrial Jobs

1133 Dundas St. E. Unit 7 & 8 (at Palston) Mississauga
(3 Stop lights west of Dixie)
Tel.: (905) 949-5083
Monday-Thursday: 9.00am to 3.00pm

PERMANENT SOLUTIONS INC.
Office Jobs

201 City Centre Drive Suite 608 Mississauga, On L5B 2T4
Tel.: (905) 566-5950 Fax: (905) 566-5991
E-mail: resumes @ permanentsolutions.com

PINSTRIPE
Office Jobs

Tel.: (905) 306-8405 Fax: (905) 306-0579
Website: www.pinstripegroup.net

PRIMARY RESPONSE INC.
Security Jobs

Fax: (416) 658-3707

PROFESSIONAL TEMPORARY SERVICES (ProTemps)
Office Jobs

Tel.: (905) 270-0022 Fax: (905) 270-4222

PROSTAFF PERSONNEL INC.
Industrial Jobs

4275 Village Centre Court Mississauga, Ontario L4Z 1V3 Tel.: (905) 279-9740 Fax:
(905) 279-1100

PROTEMPS
Office Jobs

Tel.: (905) 270-0022 Fax: (905) 270-4222

PROTEMS LITE
Temporary Industrial Jobs

151 City Centre Drive Suite 300 Mississauga
(across from Square One)

QUANTUM
Office & Industrial Jobs

33 City Cenre Dr. Suite 660C
(Across from Square One Shopping Centre) Mississauga, Ontario L5B 2N5
Tel.: (905) 276-8611
Friday: 10.00am to 3.00pm

READY STAFFING SOLUTIONS
Industrial Jobs

5170 Dixie Rd. Ste. 202 (Dixie & Aimco) Mississauga

Tel: (905) 625-4473

REQUEST PERSONNEL SERVICES INC.
Industrial Jobs

494 Brant Street Burlington, Ontario L7R 2G4
Tel.: (905) 632-4362 Brant @ caroline
420-A Britannia Road East Suite 201 Mississauga, Ontario L4Z 3L5 (Kennedy & Britannia)
Tel.: (905) 755-0395 Fax: (905) 755-0397
Website: www. Requestpersonnel.com
E-mail: requestpersonnel @ on.aibn.com

ROYAL VALVET PERSONNEL INC.
Office & Industrial Jobs

201 County Court Blvd.
Suite 502
Brampton, ON
L6W 4L2
Phone: 905-796-1136
Fax: 905-796-0321
E-mail: royalvalvet @ sprint.ca

RUSSELL STAFFING INC.
Industrial Jobs

989 Derry Rd. E. Suite 402 Mississauga
Tel.: (905) 564-9359 Fax: (905) 564-7869

SPHERTON WORKFORCE ARCHITECTS
Office Jobs

4 Robert Speck Parkway Suite 210 Mississauga, Ontario
Tel: (905) 896-1055 Fax: (905) 896-1035
Tel: (416) 259-7498 Fax: (416) 259-7669

TEAMWORK PLACEMENT INC.
Industrial Jobs

3461 Dixie Road Unit 505 (Bloor & Dixie)

THE JOB LINE
Different Jobs

24 Hours Hotline: (905) 455-4655
Website: www.thejob-line.com

THE KEITH BAGG GROUP
Office Jobs

33, City Centre Drive, Suite 580
Mississauga, Ontario
Tel: (905) 276-3940 Fax: (416) 350-9632

TODAYS STAFFING
Industrial Jobs

3300 Bloor St. W. Suite 162 (Islington & Bloor)
Tel: (416) 231-1851
Website: www.todays.com

TLCS INC.
Healthcare / Industrial / Clerical Jobs

3034 Palstan Road Unit M5
Mississauga, Ontario L4Y 2Z6
Tel: 905-273-6466
Fax: 905-273-5368
Website: www.tlcs.ca Email: recruit @ tlcs.ca

UNIQUE PERSONNEL CANADA INC.
Office Jobs

400 Creditstone Road Unit 5
Concord, Ontario L4K 3Z3
Fax: (905) 660-7581

VAN HEES PERSONNEL INC.
Industrial Jobs

115 King St. West
Dundas, Ontario
Tel: (905) 627-5472 Fax: 9905) 627-5473

E-mail: vanhees @ interlynx.net

VISIONS PERSONNEL SERVICES INC.
Industrial Jobs

Tel.: (905) 761-0566 Fax: (905) 761-8776

WILLING PERSONNEL PLUS
Industrial Jobs

1056 Wilson Ave. #100 (Keele & Wilson)
Tel.: (416) 398-3873 Fax: (416) 398-8431

APPENDIX II – Employment Agencies - Government

HUMAN RESOURCES CENTRE OF CANADA (HRCC)
A national employment service (formerly called the Canada Employment Centre)
offering assistance in the following areas:

· Employment Insurance
· Job Order Listings (Computerized Job Banks)
· Labor Market Information
· Self Employment Assistance
· Wage Subsidy Assistance Employment Information
· Human Resources Development Canada Information
· Internet site - www.the-wire.com/hrdc.html
· Application for Social Insurance Numbers

Office Hours:
Monday-Friday, 8:30 a.m.-4:00 p.m.

Location:
5343 Dundas Street W., 2nd Floor
(Dundas St. W. and Kipling Ave.)
Etobicoke, Ontario M9B 6K6

APPENDIX III – Training Information Centre (T.I.C.)

What You'll Find at the T.I.C.:

• Occupational and Career Planning Information
• Labor Market Information
• Training Information
• Job Search Information and access to the Internet
• Small Business Resources
• Community Information
• General Information Sessions on 'The Steps to Successful Training'
• and much more...

Eligibility:
No eligibility requirements. No appointment necessary.

Location:
5353 Dundas Street West, Suite 101
(Dundas St. W. and Kipling Ave.)

Hours:
Monday-Friday, 9:00 a.m.-4:00 p.m.

APPENDIX IV – Employment Resource Centers

EMPLOYMENT TOOLS:
- Access the INTERNET and BUSINESS DIRECTORIES for job leads
- Use COMPUTERS and PRINTERS to prepare your professional resume and cover letters
- Utilize the TELEPHONE to network with potential employers
- Use the FAX MACHINE to contact companies
- Learn from an extensive RESOURCE LIBRARY including books, audio cassettes, CD-ROMS, and videos

ATTEND WORKSHOPS ON:
- Effective Resume Writing
- Producing Winning Cover Letters
- Successful Interviewing Techniques
- Tapping into the 'Hidden Job Market'
- Job Searching on the Internet

ELIGIBILITY:
No eligibility requirements. No appointment necessary.

LOCATIONS/HOURS:
ETOBICOKE SOUTH
2930 Lakeshore Boulevard West
(Islington Ave. and Lakeshore Blvd. W.)
(416) 231-2295
Monday-Friday 9:00 am-5:00 pm

ETOBICOKE
5353 Dundas Street West, Suite 105
(Dundas St. W. and Kipling Ave.)
Monday-Friday 9:00 am-4:00 pm

REXDALE MICROSKILLS
1 Vulcan Street
(Martin Grove and Belfield Rd.)
(416) 247-7181
Monday, Wednesday, and Friday 8:30 am-4:30 pm Tuesday and Thursday 8:30 am-9:00 pm Saturday 10:00 am-3:00 pm

REXDALE EMPLOYMENT RESOURCE CENTRE &
THE CENTRE FOR FOREIGN TRAINED PROFESSIONALS AND TRADESPEOPLE
1620 Albion Road, 2nd Floor
(Martin Grove and Albion Rd.)
(416) 748 7200
Monday-Friday 9:00 am-4:00 pm In Partnership with Human Resources
Development Canada, and Ministry of Community and Social Services.

REXDALE YOUTH RESOURCE CENTRE
1530 Albion Road Shoppers World Albion Mall
(Kipling Ave. and Albion Rd.)
(416) 741-8714
Monday-Friday 9:30 am-4:30 pm

ELIGIBILITY:
Youth 16 - 24 years of age, living in Etobicoke

APPENDIX V – Employment Counseling Centers

The employment counselors provide free individual employment assessments that seek to identify your strengths, transferable skills, and pre-employment needs in order to chart a return-to-work action plan that will help you gain employment as soon as possible. Ongoing follow-up and support during the implementation of your action plan and afterwards is also provided.

To Access Services:
Schedule an appointment in person or over the telephone.

Locations:

1. Etobicoke Employment Counseling Centre
5353 Dundas Street West Suite 504
(Dundas St. W and Kipling Ave.)
(416) 394-4778

Eligibility:
All unemployed residents of Etobicoke who are eligible to work in Canada

Hours:
Monday to Friday, 9:00 a.rn.-4:00 p.m.

2. Rexdale Youth Resource Centre
1530 Albion Road Shoppers World Albion Mall
(Kipling Ave. and Albion Rd.)
(416) 741-8714

Eligibility:
All unemployed youth 16-24 years of age, living in Etobicoke

Hours:
Monday-Friday, 9:30 a.m.-4:30 p.m.

APPENDIX VI – Career Exploration Center

Their 2 week service will help you to:

- Identify your interests, skills, aptitudes, and work preferences through selected assessments
- Develop a personal profile for career planning
- Research occupational and training information
- Understand the labor market
- Improve your self-marketing techniques

To qualify you must meet one of the following:

- have a current claim for Employment Insurance (EI) benefits;
- have had a claim for regular benefits which ended within the previous 3 years;
- have received maternity or parental benefits within the previous 5 years and now want to return to the work force.

For referral to the next information session,
telephone (416) 394-6490

Location:
5353 Dundas Street West, Suite 501
(Dundas St. W and Kipling Ave.)
Etobicoke, Ontario
M9B 6H8

www.ingramcontent.com/pod-product-compliance
Lightning Source LLC
Chambersburg PA
CBHW060642290526
45793CB00001B/359